Rome,
A Mobile Home

Rome,
A Mobile Home

Jerry Estrin

THE FIGURES
O BOOKS
POTES & POETS
ROOF BOOKS

Copyright © 1993 by Jerry Estrin.
All rights reserved.

Design by Deborah Thomas.
Cover photograph by Norma Cole.
Author's photograph by Laura Moriarty.

ISBN: 0-937804-51-7
Library of Congress Catalog Card No.: 93-085179

Jerry Estrin wished to thank the editors of *Tramen, Ottotole, Everyday Life, Big Allis, Avec,* O Books, Potes & Poets Press, and Writing where this and other work of his appeared.

This book was published in collaboration by:
The Figures
O Books
Potes & Poets
Roof Books

Order from:
Segue Foundation
303 East 8th Street
New York, New York 10009
or
Small Press Distribution
1814 San Pablo Avenue
Berkeley, CA 94702
800/869-7553

Contents

Rome, A Mobile Home / 7

Citizen's Dash / 37

Brace / 49

Counter Song /59

Nudes / 71

Rome,
A Mobile Home

1

Between each gesture of the arm and the ball castoff to some distant alley, the eye moves still, foreigner to the other talkative physical things, the imagination of each geographic sequel and great instrumental fusion with our own piece of mirrored breathing suggesting syntactical essences:

Caesar's army Caesar's earphones Brutus's valise Caesar's saw Brutus's arrow Brutus's clothespin Caesar's pin Brutus's apple.

Planets and chairs, wheels, Caesar's syntax links up the spaces separating Roman cities, his signs hold up the stars: Sid Caesar, Jack Nicholson, Broderick Crawford, Benito Mussolini.

2

He is a smart ass. Instantly, like the illusion, his illustration vanishes. An artful mass makes him snicker, a flicker tugs at the mug of Caesar. Disrobe the images.

3

Planets and flying fish, Benito Mussolini, King Kong, the
Empire State and wheels.

Think of each thing as a world being reinvented and sincerely,
with that distant sincerity having no recognition of us

Its prehistoric attentiveness to us.

4

When you rush toward the flickering screen
The theater is missing.
Caesar expanded congruent with this space.

Of sovereignty there can be no grasp. To illustrate, one has only
to become enfranchised and utterly new, constantly there are
climate control systems in the middle of the forehead.

There are fairy tales flying into the familiar body of the empire.

. Nothingness and silence, nothing but Caesar and banks,
and banks of stars.
Were there only blank stares over Rome?

They well straight up and *enter the eradicated judges.*
Uneradicated judges enter scene by scene.

5

Increasing excitement stimulated by wounds

The gladiator becomes a pantomime

The graffiti reveals his conquests

Pulleys, racks

"pullulation of symbols devoid of significance"

Colossal bricolage (rhyme with the author?)

6

These hiding places put your children in front of you
and put my hand on their back.
You twitch for what your government might do.

I've stopped thinking, at least voluntarily.
We walk to our rooms with our measure.
I just invite you to your own pretenses.

I am using this surface repetition
but I am thinking
of what does not wear repetition away.

Control yourself.

Think of the sky and then of some sand in your hand.
We have to kill this willful technical side of ourselves to
    become dominant.
Bits of us will lament the unprotected.

7

The emperor performs by watching

The universe the night sky atop the Coliseum
This blue planet is our bath
To influence the machine

he came upon an abstraction, a system producing emperors
flat profiles, earth
undulating sentiment breezing into our little pieces of meantime.

These emperors
they think they know the end of the plot (I am you)

An ideal reconstruction of this theater.

8

Revenge
horsemanship
and epilepsy

Revenge
horsemanship
and eclipse

And the continual nervous massing of his army

9

Gaps open up in the arena.

He becomes aware he is looking at a cleverly reassembled puzzle.

The Coliseum become a maintenance center

Scene by scene, raging over the unpurchased clusters.

10

In a precise sense, the grammar of the present is equally generic.

One thinks of points in space, a man with a tree growing out of his head

At the point where the roots meet the brain

the present.

11

Under the portraits of the emperor which are stupid and heavy, seeing is dangerous because speech belongs to it. Men, philosophy, and troop strength are falling.

12

A scribe once meant a closer, as those who enclose. Hence relief, as a kind of unarmed relief pitcher, fleeing the very field of the game. Caesar say was a closer within enclosures.

He was the first fireball, always unfugitive.

History made him feel all here.

13

Printing presses and propaganda offices grace the cylinder interior. Its highest room is for bureaucrats and revolves once each month. Another is for artists, is horizontal, and revolves every day. It is an erector set. Baroque frame, glitzy, unguilty and balanced atop two lovers' heads. The red flag is our salvation. Great Lenin is dead. Repose, the exaltation of scale, the geometric purification. Lenin continues to live on thin metal in a commissar's tomb. Lenin, who used history to mean against resignation. History is what it is. Forget history. The International is our rocket ship.

14

Ideal, the emperor poses in his bridal veil
He would personify us as we resist

ourselves the phantoms of his spectacle

Lips parted, resemblance blind, unmade
according to practical terror

Recognize us, existing after
this citizen's gesture

15

Fluorescent, incandescent, and sunlight
These are sources of exhibition light
Assume responsibility as a hostage

Every image is a lone musical
Sandstone humanizes into faces
The sea fills with an artifice of light, strength and
 indifference
of sound still bordering its very traces

Proximity, following the ordinal, the measured nearness after
 daylight
Avoid those with a taste for prescription
Proximity, in the neighborhood of

Always, it is the conqueror's history which is mine
Augustus, Prince of youth
The eight divisions of the Rhine

Hebrew is the language spoken in paradise
The emperor's chariot is riderless

16

In dreams, no bystanders have faces
except we two, who still talk in rooms

of vivid rooms

The regime is overturned
The glass of the palace exploded

though now that explosion is irremediably soundless
Song by analogy

There are no masses
only ways of serving people

as masses

When our time enters history
the need for parody will become remote

17

Each no is a progress rendered by capital

A history of Kuwait, Bullion City

A history of pleasantness can be arranged

Stacks of stolen loot still steady our metaphysical Mercedes as we zoom to the border still being carried away

Bullet holes in the glass of Iraq

A politics for the present

With its repertoire

This picture is on strike

18

A line drawn in the sand, a line
To arrive, promising an endless beginning

A synchronistic citizen, a cynical
Line drawn as a calculus of transitions

A continent of time
To separate the citizens from their senses

Splendors of democracy
Plaintiffs of autonomous community

Left to gather where ever they can and will
A progression of lines forming the regular Pleiades

Fearful distances of spectacular contempt
A line of citizens, absorbed in the ubiquity

of the present trauma

Humanity and clemency to those he overpowered
Kindness to soldiers
And hearty service

Caesar killed one million Gauls
And took another one million hostage
Glory, courage, love of honor

Taut stomach
Grace and gravity
Rest in the pursuit of action

One hundred and ninety thousand nasty fighting men
These barbarians will reoccupy the very cities
    they have burnt

Weak unmanly feelings
Glory, spoils, and bodies of the slain
Where the marshes run deep and all rivers are Rubicons

Gratify Caesar
The willful universe
Relentlessly burning into the ground beneath its very
    likeness

Gratify Caesar

20

Who appointed you
To inspect the archives of the empire

"Shadow hidden in depths"
Sad mask of unrelenting ingenuousness

Holidays are days of resemblance

21

A garland of civic duty
Unguilty Catullus
And types of silence

From ambiguity to complicity

Before each ricochet you
Undo my passport, I yours,
And down we slide, stark

Naked,
Cool
Twinless

Oh,

If I believed that

22

The socratic colonnade at Alexandria
grove of the hero's lyrics

Predators or presence of verbs

Silhouettes of the Venetian sailor, the byzantine surface of the
sea ballooning up

                    Softness will come to me as my chance.

There is an interval, a caress when I say this, its delicate
fathomless distance

My heroes had no strength for this

They were the translators who made history. An inheritance

Alexander the Macedonian gangster

Alexander, Aristotle's scholar

History supernaturally signified

But the tyrant has lost his speech

              and falls into a swoon

An ancient whiteout, randomized and grave

Ahabs, with uncolonized, unindexed eyes

If there were reverse history
Many might still cite war
A still war

              this Alexandrian war

23

Predators or presence of verbs
A consummate whispering

Tempestuous agitation
Caesar is coming upon Rome

Logic masses battalions
The exiles have been called home

When the planets rise in accordance with our rest
Brutus, give this name to men

As ridicule
A sudden death is best

When you are asleep, Brutus
Sordid apocalypse

In the iconic sound of the distance
You are no longer Brutus

24

Who dreams into the dark night beyond memory
To come from nowhere as one's own ultimatum

If not for the emperor our images would knit together
Light of the day

(Truth of the world)

Troubles the infinite border that burns away
Picaresque appeal

Prey of history
Alexandria

Spoils to friends
And Homer's *Iliad* which he kept in a booty casket

False perfection
Duplicitous story

Lebenswelt (living world)
Silence only where it is

Face with roots in facade
Defenseless face

Sovereign instant
Silence so windy in its cells

25

Lights of the far-off town
Light an indescribable index

Figures of smoke trouble the infinite
Border that burns away

Picturesque appeal
Prey of history

Instinct for sovereignty
Preying on history

Stoic irregular sangfroid
Theater of lives

Apocalyptic anonymous flight
On frightened Puritanic sands

Instinctual separation near burden of asylum

Citizen's Dash

1

What words are not pure
There was a robbery
Hollow, but tainted by conversation
An enclosure soaring in mist
No courage from the scattering
If to surrender to it
Benediction verbatim
Fictional predestination
Flesh and wheel

2

Light outsideless and yet pervading
Ghosts of Vermeer's light
Collected by princes

Faces lit from the left
Passivity and withdrawal
The full provenance

Prized by connoisseurs
Censored, revelatory
A metropolis for disconnected citizens

Cons
This human dimension
Who keeps up a processional tension

Imperial decay
Uncontrollable at the edge
Framed sanctuary or the fame of it

3

Writing covers the citizen's body
A terrible mockery
Tuned to transport zones

Distant blaze, untemporalized
Jingle
To hold off estrangement

With the frozen infatuation
Of zero

Army of armies

4

The boys from Warsaw, a kind of collective madness
Wouldn't interfere, were already sacred
Death to private booty, collective spoils

An impossible poetry, an irreducible existence
Removed Arabs from land to found a Kibbutz for Jews
Choleric null point propped against onslaught

A silent call, a theater
Irreducible to gesture
Couldn't speak, were already elsewhere

5

The law, which convulses the body
As in birth
Precarious and final
Vertigo forms the ground of the pursuer
Figure and ground Medusa headed
Marble columned walking courts receding to infinity
The exhilarated realist
Lights the courtyard
Candelabra from illusionary rooms
Penetrator or penetratee
The court a conjurer's marble sea
The familiarity of repose

6

And it's late summer, light
Grey to pearl, a vibration

Dissolved in light,
Our lips parted in a private

Tango —

Unforseen
Vibration of control

Palette for random
Others who colors

This horizon-
Less me

You and this edge-
Less indifference.

7

    The girl, moving, one knee up, circling, on the hill in the wind — in the wind by the bulldozed schoolyard, aware and yet not caring that I have seen her — while below the turmoil of the city, ships at anchor, rush-hour . . .

        Circle the hill in the wind
        By the bulldozer by the schoolyard
        Autonomous within your reverie

        White hills cancelled by color
        Inward cakes of creamy nothing
        Ramshackle rush-hour and yourself a souvenir

        Inviolable (and only here?) adrift in the glare

8

Magnificent pink roses, chrysanthemums in a Greek vase, the color spectrum's rhetoric in an untranslated book, apocalyptic wallpaper for the chessroom. Patience. There is a comet tail, a yellowish drip of unconscious brush stroke to the right. Have a drink. Blackness is before you and black is your favorite color. Honk. A customer will haul the installation away. Even now this gravedigger cruises on an ocean liner. He teeters on the edge of your work. Objects unrecognize you. The East is empty, there is nothing left to the West except the past, which is a groundless night, a mass solution (like panic) to solitude, an imperishable escape. Let's go to Paris. Let's live, therefore we'll think. We'll be admitted to the best seats at the Opera, indicted for treason, encouraged to seduce our new enemies, become diplomats, say grace with the trackless courtesans. There are dull beatitudes and reanimated brains. Houdini. The art of dissemination is the sign of the prodigy.

Citizen's Dash

He needs the job, but wants the woman. That is ambiguous, since he can't be here, in L. A., and here, outside of Reno, now and then. He needs a drink, but dust covers the dash. The desert fills up the window, the town goes on, hot and circular, then there is more dust, sheer drifts of colors, and a band, which is hot too, playing a fast kind of banged-up shiny margin, less serene than a world, tangible, as an immediate scar. The end of this serenity has no name, no grade, but plenty of occasional ambiguity. He finishes the job, the unfinished world, but the pose isn't free. Too set, too four, the hieroglyphic is the equivalent of the movie house. Each flicker holds up its tomorrow, its lived, its resplendent inertia. A slow roar kicks up dust around the ferris wheel. The black alabaster tablecloth covers no table but a cube. An eerie resemblance winks at this picture, then puts him and it, the table, back together. A restoration of contact. The contract crowds the moment. A head, his, turns, follows an hour, falling place. It is unbeguiled, this falling place, a gravity cluster. He finds some found footage, swims in it, splashes with brilliant red, refuses to merge with the blueness of shore. The shore is the eye of talk, endlessly it fuses with someone's soliloquy. Its skin is repose. He walks, up and into poses, multiplying into cities of domes, pyramids, complex miraged shelters that disappear into water. The landscape is uncolorized, advisorless, as the last, the last picture book. He marches across this horizonless map. There is a river, or what is left of it, a treacherous bridge. He puts that together with what he sees fit. Monopoly, self-mastery, a sometimes funny incongruity. Flares go off in the daze, questions light up the solo armor. He is unrehearsed stark merchandise, never mind make believe. He carves up this everyday belief into witnesses with temporary parallels. Its traces are testaments falling away from order. Unweighted, unravelling, inevitable, he turns around, he looks out a window. Vanishing points mutiny, absorb his constant glance. The citizens dash, rumoring an absence charged with a touch of babel. The air is criminal, without consonance, impossible to imitate. He says hello, offers this word for the world, free of rent, even when surrounded by it.

BRACE

Brace

During the 1961 season, Roger Maris broke Babe Ruth's home-run record. At the conclusion of his final home run, Maris cried: I've taken my last swing, I am finished. I will now be visible forever.

Diary: the grass on the field, the stands, heavy with fans, the press corps, high in the stands, and Maris, connecting with the pitch, the ball, soaring over the center-field wall . . .

Maris, striking the ball, gives the home run its form.

People running, the ball, invisible, in the single movement of the swing . . .

Perfection of the swing, white-out of the ball, a surfeit never extinguished, asymmetrical to the distant epiphany of its form.

Crowds intensely draw all stories to themselves, are capable of any form. Violence of the swing, then a roar.

Without inside, Maris, after his final hit, would not speak, or rather, there was the sight of his swing, caught on camera, repeating itself, forever.

Maris' swing, its constancy.

Night, Maris, under Yankee Stadium light, the crowd.

The crash of the ball, and Maris, caught in that instant, without inside, opening, to the evening.

Goodbye, he says through the night of the stadium air.   Ah, I am finished.

Duration of the game, a player's ration.

Image of Maris, flap of pinstripes, under shadowless stadium light.

Image before, Maris at the plate, bat about to explode into ball.

The roar, the sound of bat on ball. The swing never post-game

but prior to definition, to description

to our agitation.

Repose, words of prose, existing once and for all, removed from bat and ball.

Lights of the far-off town
L.A. burning away.

On the far edge of the park
they shout U.S.A.! U.S.A!

Now and before
the game returning to itself.

Wrong game.

Unflappable, unfathomed
Maris multiplies daily.

I go to the park, to watch the A's
make contact (the Oakland A's).

A line drive cannot help or hurt.
But a line from Zukofsky's *"A"* – 23?

He is where.

Death to the commissioner
when Maris kills the pitch.

Lebenswelt
The ball lost in the sun.

Maris

A spectral mosaic

Suffused by our thought of him

Whose swing divorced from anything

Roger, plaintiff of our autonomous community

In the major leagues

The ballpark lights go on and off

An impossible catch

A seventh-inning stretch

Déjà vu.

I mean what the stars have to sell is their autonomy

Maris, his oxygenated simplicity.

Think of a film, an unmoving Roger Maris, whose doll eyes never flicker. Shot of the street, of rhythmical crowds, of Roger there.

Maris the modernist, sufficient to himself, has become the paradoxical hero of an instant that endures without a future.

Counter Song

The Park

The studio, its war films, its triangular affairs, quits thought with lecherous kaleidoscopes. The park, northeast beyond the irrigation ditches and the orange trees. Or the frontier then, along with some angels falling from the limbo of concrete. We take for granted, finally, this subjective wandering in the mathematics of total force, the generative steel. Unapproachable, cordoned off zones, unpenetrated flash of indeterminate milieus, paradoxically living. That's that. Is that in the park?

*

Anonymity (history), common sense, scattering a landscape of numbers: five hundred fifty . . . eight hundred . . . ten million . . . seventy-five thousand.

The sheet music is original, not the music but its alteration.

He was reading the fluctuations of the stock market (allegory: a whole which shelters us).

Or: The moon above the meadow unpersuaded by this luscious illustration: so utterly feigned, commensurate with a trustworthiness which costumes the citizens; uncalculated, a moon, approaching pines on a mountain, below which, close to a window, he suddenly turns in the night to see, missing from those features — that there should properly be huge exhumed tunnels, holes in the conduit, we two climbing out, even the costumes of these citizens reflecting, contributing to the construction of a world utterly unfeigned, incommensurate.

Thus the evidence obliges an existence between, an identity, an ongoing effigy.

*

But when I crossed the frontier, I walked across the street and into the park. More than my house I need the truth of this park, I thought. But my house without a park I need too.

*

Orphan territory.
The park, dreaming of fountains, useless play
The park, where I find myself mirrored

*

What you see before you is the Seagram Building, New York City. Withdrawn from the kaleidoscopic image tank of the city, aloof, present in the particularity of its steel columns (its steel skeleton) and glass cover wall (its multi-directional reflecting skin), autonomous and yet proposing, through its reflecting and yet nearly transparent facades, its combination of tremendous verticality and near emptiness, its permutating mullions, its cleared space around its own staged structural foregrounding and perfection, the Seagram Building exists to be performed, dematerializing into a process of design supplied and completed by the man on the street. The citizen confronts the Seagram Building. The Seagram Building confronts the citizen. Utterly rational structural organization proposes its dialogue. A critical space, a subversive theater, an art abandoning its aura, vanishes into the politics of everyday life.

*

... A photograph of Huntington Park, the drinking fountain, with its consistency of emphasis, its metamorphic if polyphonic battlescapes imported from Rome, reportedly saved from Mussolini's bulldozers — what bulldozed memories, as some indestructible finger-painted colony, as the earthquake pinkness of the jukebox sense of this light in the park. Lead banners which resemble no presentiment, no each time. What rhyme isn't so feigned? Homage to the view? Or to perdition, only precision surviving.

Sing my astronaut suit.

Counter Song

Damaged Frames (holes in the museum roof), the
 whispering
of the background whoosh.
A performance, the fortress of the person on stage.

There is science fiction.
There is an outlawed transmission.
Our bodies outwallop any transmission.

There is movement on Tuesday, budget codes and
 responsibility
of your thighs, unprincipled, uncompleted surplus, the
sources our principles are our red revenue sources,
 accumulating.

Laws are feigned, oedipal.
Each law of contempt implies its opposite, nightingale.
I can lie in your sense or between your teeth.

The idea of nature is transformed.
There is foliage and the wind and fucking, shades
of landlords, charity

concerns us.
This is in real time, and no long range.
There is Tuesday, budget codes and responsibility.

Incongruent crisis management —
A system of blues lies under you.
Arrangements of contractual gestures.

The park is uninhabitable.
The soul is unfathomable, a deep peach
of dream speech ensnares depth.

Each curling flower is between spaces.

Amphetamine has smoked marijuana.
Flares are the early Renaissance, the eye.

Bush Street is near Montgomery Street Chinatown.
The junta is in Chile.
People have often said the city when they meant
    capitalism.

Consider the park as an order of language, a green.
Israel knows what God is from what He is doing
    in history.
A man is dancing to static or he is being shot.

Our static is rich
a point of view
Your point of view doesn't belong to you.

Humans are traitors to their species.
Random violets in the park.
Park a premeditated park.

*

One makes a portrait, perhaps empty, of fated being, in resistance to a crushing symbolic order. Writing takes its primary measure of this constricted, if artifacted space and time. A phantom order empowers its own existence. It is a hope, or a false utopia, a neutral territory, a blank milieu.

*

There are a hundred sonic booms in the valley a day, the
    people.
They are camping on bombing ranges, the people.
The land is legal because it is contaminated.

You find yourself in a position of power.
You can think, the land is regal.
You are participating in reality.

They have prejudices against artists.
Seeds of scurvy — grass growing in waterpots.
Their rooms are filled to excess with art objects.

The book the just language
of the park, one more metaphor or another,
spills

reverses its horizon into me.
Cite the way why
argue it, those wise don't

inflict your living this place
simple, quiet, kind.
There is no neutral landscape.

These facts have to do with the truth.
Do you believe in the truth.
We admire the brilliance of the least fact that happens.

Believe in the porosity of the existing situation.
The light is incessant, the eternal
spring enamels everything.

A park comes into view only for you.
We have worries.
We have the same reasons we had in 1929

to flee from reality.
Visualize the poem's door.
In which sun are you asleep.

We are fascinated by an absence of totality.
If anguish is embedded in the territory.
If there is no Palestinian territory.

There is fate.
We will be acting out your comments.
That which never has preexisted.

The snares are relentless among the worldly.
If the air in the city has preexisted this city.
If the park is an ongoing effigy

Our words are not autonomous.
I speak
like all your friends

or any of your friends talk.
Talk.
Talk makes me feel first class.

Thanks Merrill Lynch and Co.
I know this ironic time
and that this line

is leering at us.
Us fears are their features our
futures have become mutants

because all future representations are futile.
Save the box and the memo preserving it.
Preserve what has prolonged you.

I should be your comments
to transmute an education.
We should fuck and fuck

because we will all be literal when we fuck.
Fantasy is clipped from living material.
Responsibility is unjustifiable.

The verdant fountain of the Tuileries.
In the park the fountain.
There are obstacles and malevolences

which are contradictions.
There is the board of trustees.
Bequests of land round the capitol.

If there are enough caricatures
There will be an equivalence
of distortion.

Listen on Friday we will get metaphysical.
We will send the document to planned parenthood.
Wilderness in the notes.

The Capitol is alive, harmony
keeps acquiring our targets The park
Responsibility is unjustifiable.

Separations are our responsibility.
My airfare I'll be sending you.
Keep silence. Silence cannot be kept.

Check.
Their documents are secret.
All documents are secret.

Who is organizing this surrealist show?
Our parallels are secret.
Fall into the person you are

an endless suffusion, profusion.
In the mountains drive fast.
True intelligence would be to flood

an enemy with true intelligence.
Torture his linear consistency.
At the border visit the rides

like Walter Benjamin
with frictional curiosity
one can cancel

an interval in Mecca
caress injuries
teach

        each creature to be a monument
        calling through time.
        In the park a stone fountain

        weeping out our years.
        Our union exists
amid permanent damage to the replica.

NUDES

1

To emerge from power as a ghost
With one knee held out to stage light
To stage light
The ghost of a line
An analogy can hardly be conceived
With one's own will
One is turned or returned upon one's own kind
Or finding kindness
Reinvented
In toneless colors
Comprehensible because outside
A kind if comfortless
Ghost of a line
Of self-professed access
This shattered figure of victory

2

He falls out of the world unconfronted
A wordless body

Unwritten by words
The body floating indifferently

To its shuddering narrative
The body receding

To why me where the words lie
And what why me, stuttering

Uncoerced, unrehearsed, his
Sense broken open

3

Here the old swim toward their youth.

    The Gothic

deploys uniform light as a gift

    yet masks
    witnesses to their own resemblances.

Illuminated old people

    flung back their hair, floated
    bellyward toward their youth.

Then gave up the long habit of living.

4

But of models now

    Or stages

Inherited from our fathers, mathematics

I have this ideal I should live forever

Idols which are dispersed, eyeless

Words whose untrapped means

    The stucco nude

    The stone nude

5

Sol justitiae

The crushing strength of a body

On a rock intoning in beefy darkness

Its impervious gesture

6

I imagine the setting for a spy novel, the assassin in the idling car, the passerby having escaped his victimhood, yet the killers are relentless, insisting even on the scenery projected by me, I who have become the one they are pursuing. Perhaps this scene requires particulars, formulaic, silent: 'his' overcoat hanging in an open closet, some books which 'represent' him:

A dignity astonished by my last grasp at personhood — or the absence of a nostalgia only I could write.

7

The powers of order are never naive
Power works by normalization

Breathing protest
You touch me

To heal disintegration
A necessary social facade

An indecently marble ankle
(Sensuality heals disintegration)

So I will be gorgeous
If to contaminate

This angle for the rarified
Certain to shed public blood

For realists and their gross appetites
Dissolution cannot be predicted

Belly and thighs expose an interval
A system of arabesques

Poisoned by impatience, then
Patience comes due

8

New features and details emerge

The one hesitating in her *Odalisque*
Because stripped of her materiality

Stoicism of unironic singularity

The one trembling inside these lines
Seeking these essential lines

Dishonest
The essential lies

The one serenity, emerging
From color: pink then peacock blue

Enjoyable totalities

Ovals, ellipsoids and spheres
Are inhumanly modest

Because inhuman

Silence's injunction
Essential to play with insecurity

Sandwiched between collective vacancies
No difference

And on the "French grass" he painted her

9

Measured riches
Where between us lies

To be overwhelmed by what
Is not in us to control

Cloud
Painted to the receding ceiling

Your face
Awaiting pleasure

Your body's silence
(no anecdote)

Born in Los Angeles in 1947, Jerry Estrin grew up playing in the back lots of movie studios. He received a B.A. in Russian History and Sociology from UCLA, an M.A. in Literacy Education from UC Berkeley, and an M.A. in English from San Francisco State. He variously drove a cab and did a stint maintaining the kettle at Anchor Steam Beer. He worked for many years in the director's office of the University Art Museum at Berkeley. As founder and editor of the magazines *Vanishing Cab* and *Art and Con*, Estrin was one of the west coast's most influential editors. He and his wife, the writer Laura Moriarty, were together for 19 years. He spent his last year finishing *Rome, A Mobile Home*. Jerry died at home of adrenal cancer on June 22, 1993.

His books include *A Book of Gestures* (Sombre Reptiles, 1980), *In Motion Speaking* (Chance Additions, 1986) and *Cold Heaven* (Zasterle Press, 1990).